IMPRESSIVE advertising
Copyright © 2017 Instituto Monsa de ediciones

Editor, concept, and project director
Anna Minguet

Co-autor
Miquel Abellán

Project's selection, design and layout
Miquel Abellán (Monsa Publications)
Cover design
Eva Minguet (Monsa Publications)

Image pages 2-3 by CLM BBDO
Image pages 142-143 by Lapizdebits

INSTITUTO MONSA DE EDICIONES
Gravina 43 (08930)
Sant Adrià de Besòs
Barcelona (Spain)
Tlf. +34 93 381 00 50
www.monsa.com
monsa@monsa.com

Visit our official online store!
www.monsashop.com

Follow us on facebook!
facebook.com/monsashop

ISBN: 978-84-16500-41-3
D.L. B 1397-2017
Printed by Impuls45

By Miquel Abellán

IMPRESSIVE advertising

monsa

Intro

Impressive advertising

A visual and emotional impact, etc... the key to many campaigns, and the essential element for reaching the widest possible audience, generating a whole range of sensations in the viewer.
A successful advertising campaign, via its script and presentation, needs to stand out amid hundreds of other received images, and manage to ensure that is more memorable and visible than the rest. To achieve this it must impact on the senses after first capturing our attention through surprise, intrigue, curiosity, and sometimes even via negative sensations such as disgust, rejection or an appeal to the conscience. All sorts of emotional responses may be affected by a well planned publicity campaign, leaving the viewer with a strong sense of the specific and desired message.

We have looked at two particular chapters in the book, "Printed Advertising", which presents a range of work produced for media such as magazines, newspapers, brochures, mailbox leaflets and mailing..., in short all types of advertising on paper, as well as "Outdoor Advertising", in which public spaces are used to display messages to an undetermined audience.

El impacto visual, emocional, etc... la clave de muchas campañas, conseguir comunicar al mayor público posible, generando sensaciones de todo tipo en el receptor.
Una campaña de publicidad, a través de un guión argumental, tiene que destacar entre centenares de inputs, conseguir ser única y más visible que el resto, para ello es necesario impactar sensorialmente, después de haber captado nuestra atención con sorpresa, intriga, curiosidad, o a veces incluso generando impresiones negativas como repulsión, rechazo o un toque de atención a la conciencia. Todas las emociones pueden alterarse detrás de una buena campaña publicitaria, dejando en el receptor un mensaje concreto, el mensaje deseado.

Encontramos dos capítulos en el libro, "Publicidad Impresa", que nos acerca a diferentes trabajos realizados para medios como revistas, periódicos, panfletos, folletos de buzoneo o de mailing..., en definitiva, sobre papel, y "Publicidad de Exterior" en la que se utilizan lugares públicos para desarrollar y esta dirigida a un público indeterminado.

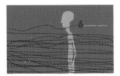

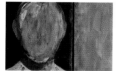

Printed
Advertising

"Publicidad Impresa"

Printed advertising is that produced for media such as magazines, newspapers, brochures, mailbox leaflets and mailing..., in short, on paper.
Creativity is a key factor in current advertising and communication. In a world where the user receives a vast range of visual stimuli every second, advertising designers and copywriters need to continually devise ways of making the message both attractive and memorable, as the first step that will inspire the decision making process leading to the purchase of the product.

Advertising which fails to transmit a message is instantly forgettable and will not have an impact. On the other hand a simple advertising idea, which nevertheless makes the customer think and relate to the concept in some way, will be vastly more effective.

We will go on to present various examples of printed advertising which some of the leading agencies have personally selected for inclusion in the book.

La publicidad impresa es la que se realiza en medios como revistas, periódicos, panfletos, folletos de buzoneo o de mailing..., en definitiva, sobre papel.
La creatividad es un factor clave en la comunicación y publicidad actuales. Ante un mundo en el que el usuario recibe una cantidad enorme de estímulos visuales por segundo. Los creativos publicitarios deben ingeniárselas para que la comunicación resulte atractiva, memorable e incite a dar los primeros pasos en el proceso de toma de decisiones hacia la compra del producto.

La publicidad que no cuenta nada, no es memorable y no causa ningún impacto. Al contrario, una pieza publicitaria sencilla, pero que haga pensar mínimamente al cliente, que lo haga ser partícipe de nuestra historia será mas efectiva.

A continuación las agencias mas destacadas nos presentan diferentes trabajos de publicidad impresa, que han seleccionado específicamente para el libro.

Leo Burnett

Frankfurt ◊ Germany
PRINT

Marketing Florian Zimmermann
Chief Creative Officer Andreas Pauli
Creative Director Copy Jörg Hoffmann
Creative Director Art Daniela Ewald
Art Till Rothweiler
ACD Designer Hugo Moura
Copywriter Andreas Daum
Photographer Miro Minarovych

For Those Who Hate Going Twice

Frankfurt am Main, June 24th 2016. Leading advertising agency Leo Burnett was honored with a Silver Cannes Lion award for work on behalf of Fiat Professional at the Cannes Lions International Festival of Creativity in Cannes, France. For the "For Those Who Hate Going Twice" campaign Leo Burnett created three motives that won in the category Print and Publishing.
The posters reflect a situation everybody knows: When you have to bring many items from one place to another, you rather carry everything at once by stacking everything in an almost artistic way instead of going twice. This insight is as true for craftsmen, construction workers and people owning small businesses - the clients of Fiat Professional. With this series of magazine ads Leo Burnett demonstrated the load capacity of the Fiat Ducato in a surprising way that everybody can relate to.

Frankfurt am Main, 24 de junio de 2016. La destacada agencia de publicidad Leo Burnett ha sido galardonada con el León de Plata por su trabajo para Fiat Professional en el Festival Internacional de Creatividad Cannes Lions de Cannes, Francia. Para su campaña "For Those Who Hate Going Twice" (Para los que odian ir dos veces) Leo Burnett creó tres motivos ganadores de la categoría Print and Publishing (Anuncio impreso y editorial).
Los pósteres reflejan una situación que todo el mundo conoce: Cuando tenemos que llevar muchas cosas de un lugar a otro y lo hacemos de una sola vez apilando unos objetos encima de otros de manera casi artística en vez de recorrer el camino dos veces. Esta situación la viven también los artesanos, trabajadores de la construcción y propietarios de pequeñas empresas, clientes de Fiat Professional. Con esta serie de anuncios para revista, Leo Burnett demuestra la capacidad de carga de la Fiat Ducato de un modo sorprendente en el que todo el mundo puede verse reflejado.

FOR THOSE WHO HATE GOING TWICE
FIAT DUCATO

FOR THOSE WHO HATE GOING TWICE
FIAT DUCATO

FOR THOSE WHO HATE GOING TWICE
FIAT DUCATO

Michurin

Kiev ◊ Ukraine
PRINT

Creative Director Irina Metneva
Account Manager Liza Levchenko
Producer Tatyana Rudenko
Post Production Looma
Art Director Sergey Prokopchuk
Dop Sergey Prokopchuk
Photographer Igor Bogun

Play with beauty

Sister's Market – is an ambitious cosmetics marketplace based in Kiev. The idea of campaign is based on insight – cosmetics are the women's toys, just like a lovely Teddy bear.

Sister's Market - es un ambicioso mercado de cosméticos con sede en Kiev. La idea de la campaña se basa en la visión - de los cosméticos como juguetes para las mujeres, simulando un precioso osito de peluche.

Y&R

São Paulo ◊ Brazil
PRINT

Chief Creative Officer Rui Branquinho
Head of Art Felipe Pavani
Creative Director Rui Branquinho
Art Director Denon Figueiredo, Silas Nogueira, Eduardo Araujo
Copywriter Rui Branquinho, Flavio Cherem
Illustrators Marcelo Braga, Estúdio Notan
Photography Marcus Hausser
Art Buyer Monica Beretta, Stephanie Wang
Print Production Ronaldo Cavalcante
Client Services Vivianne Brafmann, Heloisa Guimarães
Media Gustavo Gaion, Marcello Bolla

Chroma Key

To remind people that publishing house Penguin has great classics in its portfolio, we have created a campaign in which we show characters from renowned classic literary titles covered by Chroma key fabric.
Only one distinguishing prop of those characters was not part of the cinematographic effect that, in our campaign, represents the readers' imagination and their unique ways of imagining the details of each story.
The pieces also contain hand-designed titles and frames with typography and shapes that better represent each tale and key elements present in the stories.

Para recordar a la gente que la editorial Penguin cuenta con grandes clásicos en su catálogo, hemos creado una campaña en la que se muestran personajes de conocidas obras clásicas cubiertos con tela de croma.
Sólo una parte característica de estos personajes no se ha incluido en el efecto cinematográfico que, en nuestra campaña, representa la imaginación del lector y su forma única de imaginar los detalles de cada historia.
Las piezas contienen además títulos diseñados a mano y fotogramas con las tipografías y formas que mejor representan cada relato y elemento fundamental presente en cada historia.

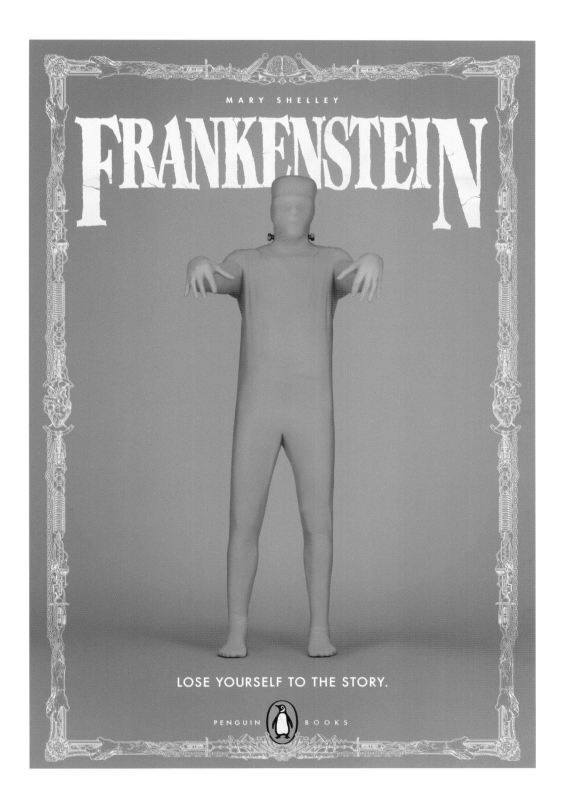

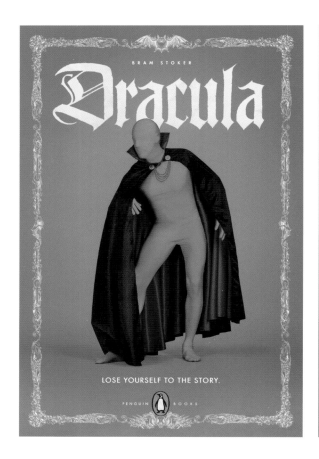

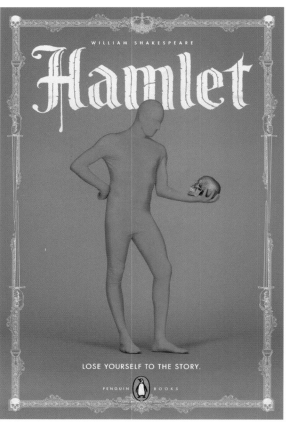

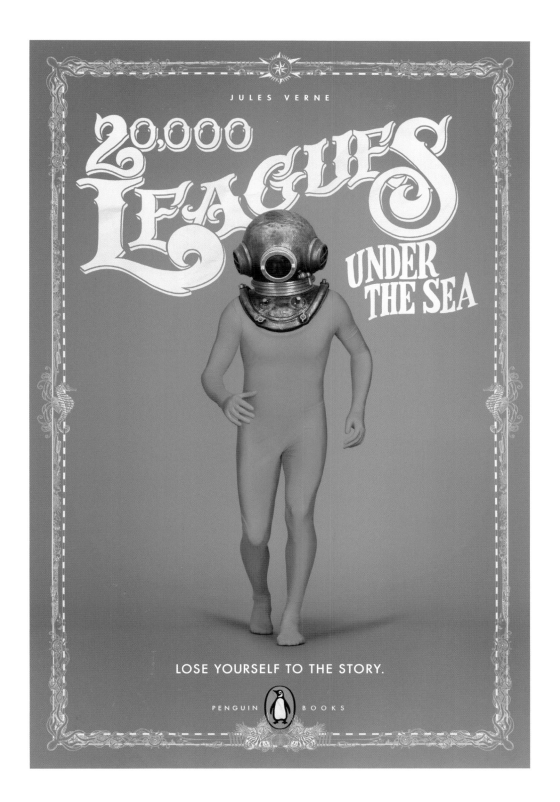

Ogilvy & Mather

Frankfurt ◊ Germany
PRINT

Chief Creative Officer Dr. Stephan Vogel
Creative Director Helmut Meyer, Lothar Mueller
Art Director Jawad Saleem
Copywriter Lothar Mueller
Account Management Michael Fucks
Advertiser's Supervision Marcel Hagmann
Illustrator Jawad Saleem
Media Planner Patricia Gottet/Mindshare Zurich

End Inhumanity

Human rights are under huge pressure. Against the backdrop of the refugee crisis in Europe and the increasing number of states where human rights are violated Amnesty Switzerland wanted to raise awareness for human rights. With a poster campaign for citylight posters in Switzerland.
The hope Amnesty means to many victims of suppression around the globe is symbolized in the Amnesty brand logo: candle and barbwire. We used it to make clear what Amnesty could be one day if more people join it: the point where inhumanity ends.
Jawad Saleems incredibly emotional illustrations for the campaign express Amnesty's core idea in a totally disarming way – they are silently screaming out amnesty's key message: There is hope, if we stand up together.

End inhumanity!

Los derechos humanos se encuentran bajo una enorme presión. Ante el telón de fondo de la crisis de refugiados que vive Europa y el creciente número de países donde se violan los derechos humanos, Amnistía Internacional Suiza ha querido aumentar la concienciación sobre dichos derechos humanos. Para ello ha creado una campaña para carteles luminosos de la ciudad que se ha implementado en Suiza. Mediante el logo de la organización, una vela y alambre de púas, se representa la esperanza que Amnistía Internacional busca para las víctimas de represión de todo el mundo. Éste se ha utilizado para dejar claro lo que podría llegar a ser Amnistía Internacional si más gente se uniese a ella: el punto en el que termina la crueldad.
Las increíblemente emocionales ilustraciones de Jawad Saleems para la campaña expresan la idea principal de Amnistía Internacional de un modo totalmente cautivador: con gritos en silencio del mensaje clave de Amnistía Internacional: Existe esperanza, si nos levantamos juntos.

¡Pongamos fin a la crueldad!

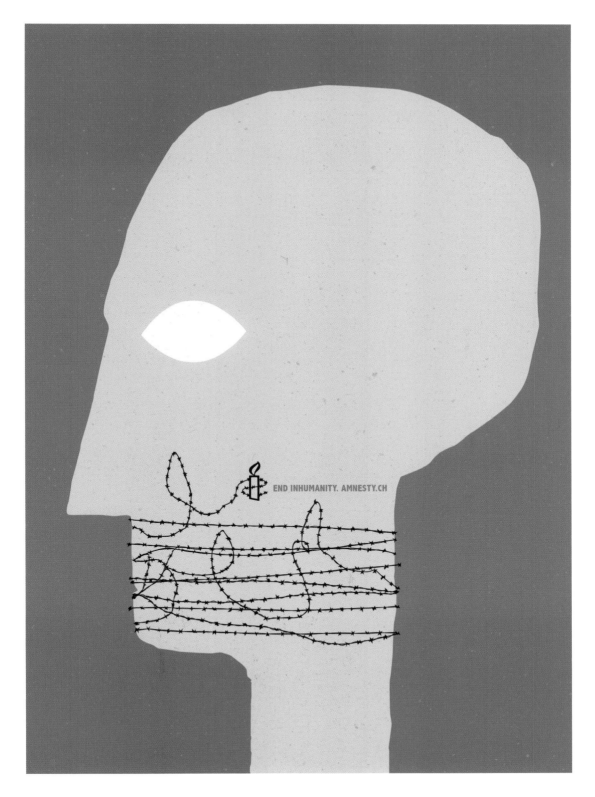

END INHUMANITY. AMNESTY.CH

23

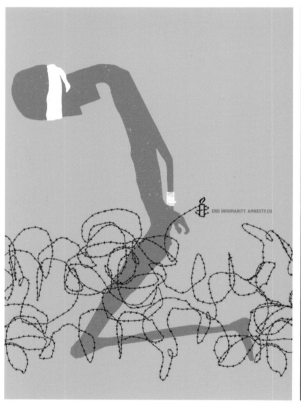

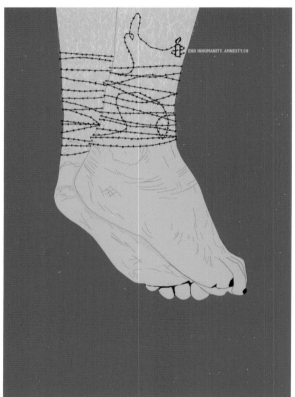

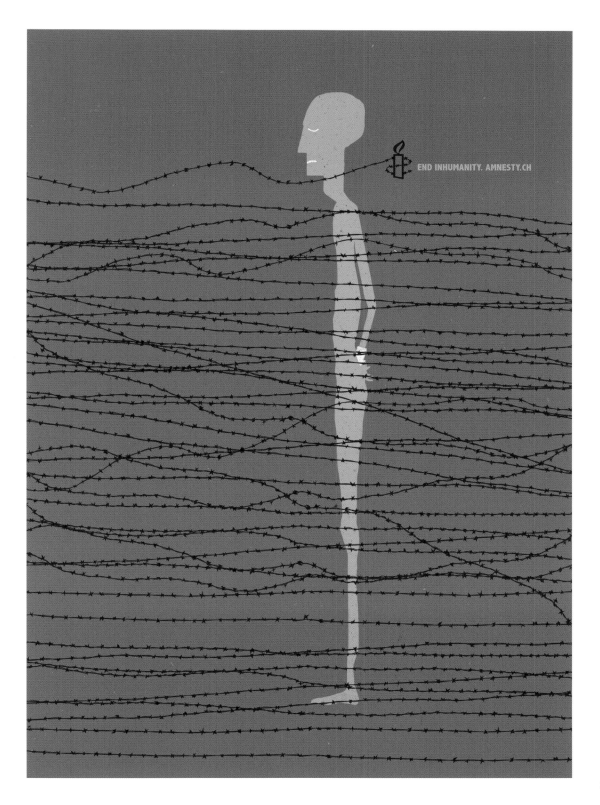

END INHUMANITY. AMNESTY.CH

Saatchi & Saatchi Wellness

New York ◊ USA
PRINT

Chief Creative Officer Kathy Delaney
Creative Director Carol Fiorino
Art Director Carolyn Gargano
Copywriter Scott Carlton
Photographer Erik Almas
Account Director Rob Galimidi
Account Supervisor Angela Dawson
Strategic Planning Marcia Gold

Allergan:
Lifting the burden

Women who are diagnosed with Chronic Migraine have a terrible burden to bear each day. They hurt badly – so badly that simply turning their heads can feel like being sideswiped by a heavy object.
But Chronic Migraine sufferers are strong. No matter what their pain, they power on. So we thought why not tap into their fighting spirits with a provocatively visual approach?
Showing them standing tall, this unbranded print campaign informed women of new ways to help lift the burden of Chronic Migraine.

Las mujeres a las que se les diagnostica migraña crónica soportan una terrible carga cada día. La migraña es muy dolorosa, tanto que sólo girar la cabeza es como si nos golpeasen con un objeto pesado.
Pero las personas que padecen migraña crónica son fuertes. Independientemente del dolor, se ponen en marcha. De ahí que pensásemos en despertar su espíritu luchador con un acercamiento visual provocador.
Mostrando a las mujeres en lo alto, esta campaña impresa sin marca pretendía informar a las mismas de nuevas formas de ayuda para soportar la carga de la migraña crónica.

CHRONIC MIGRAINE
DOESN'T HAVE TO FLATTEN ME

Discover treatment options and ways to manage your Chronic Migraine.
If you're getting hit by migraines with 15 or more headache days a month, each lasting 4 hours or more, talk to a headache specialist and learn how you can fight back. Visit us online.

MYCHRONICMIGRAINE.COM

CHRONIC MIGRAINE
DOESN'T HAVE TO DERAIL ME

Discover ways to manage your Chronic Migraine.
If you're getting hit by migraines with 15 or more headache days a month,
each lasting 4 hours or more, talk with your doctor, and visit us online to fight back.

myChronicMigraine.com

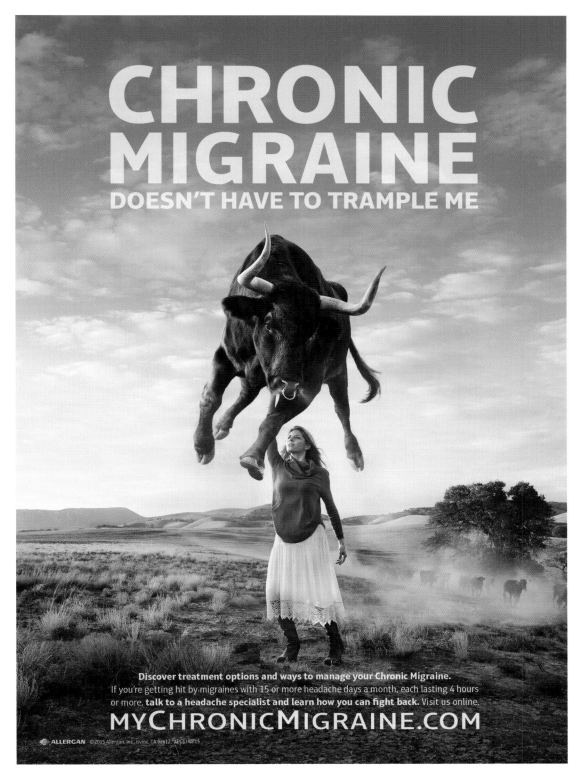

CHRONIC MIGRAINE
DOESN'T HAVE TO TRAMPLE ME

Discover treatment options and ways to manage your Chronic Migraine.
If you're getting hit by migraines with 15 or more headache days a month, each lasting 4 hours or more, **talk to a headache specialist and learn how you can fight back.** Visit us online.

MYCHRONICMIGRAINE.COM

New !

New York ◊ USA
PRINT

Chief Creative Officer Kathy Delaney
Creative Director Carol Fiorino
Art Director Carolyn Gargano
Copywriter Scott Carlton
Photographer Erik Almas
Account Director Rob Galimidi
Account Supervisor Angela Dawson
Strategic Planning Marcia Gold

Mint Vinetu
Give a newlife

A book is only alive when it is read. So we invite people to bring their dusty old classics and give new life for hemingways, twains or shakespeares. For somebody this will be a huge find, an amazing encounter. We show very literally how newborn Ernest, Mark & William would look like.

And who can resist the selling power of the kids, right? Even if they have moustache.

Un libro sólo cobra vida cuando se lee. Por eso invitamos a la gente a traer sus viejos y polvorientos clásicos y dar una nueva vida a sus hemingways, twains o shakespeares. Para alguien serán un gran hallazgo, un increíble descubrimiento. Mostramos de manera muy literal el aspecto que tendrían Ernest, Mark y William recién nacidos.

¿Y quién se puede resistir al poder de venta de los niños? Aunque tengan bigote.

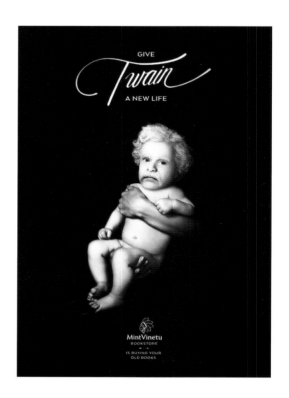

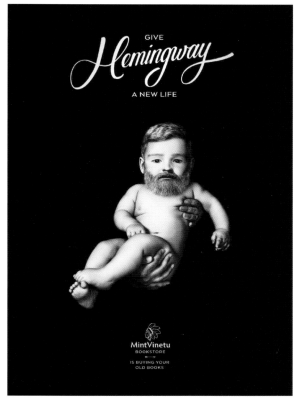

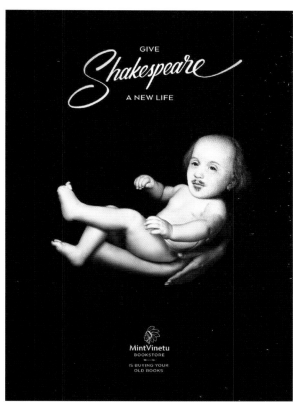

Lapizdebits

Bogotá ◊ Colombia
PRINT

Creative Director Artiom Gelvez Kostenko
Art Director Artiom Gelvez Kostenko
Copywriter Alex Valyukh
Illustrator Artiom Gelvez Kostenko

WWF
Green / Blue

One out – all down

WWF

Leo Burnett

Frankfurt ◊ Germany
PRINT

Creative Director Hans-Juergen Kaemmerer
Art Directors Christopher Bueers, David Apel
Copywriter Florian Fehre
Photography Getty Images, Gorka Aranzabal
Modelling Johannes Brus, Patric Rottenecker

Frankfurt Zoological Society

The amount of statues already outnumbers their living relatives. Help us preserve wild animals and their natural habitat.

La cantidad de estatuas ya supera a sus parientes vivos. Ayúdenos a preservar los animales salvajes y en su hábitat natural.

THE AMOUNT OF STATUES ALREADY OUTNUMBERS THEIR LIVING RELATIVES.
Protect wild animals and their natural habitat: fzs.org
FRANKFURT ZOOLOGICAL SOCIETY

THE AMOUNT OF STATUES ALREADY OUTNUMBERS THEIR LIVING RELATIVES.
Protect wild animals and their natural habitat: fzs.org
FRANKFURT ZOOLOGICAL SOCIETY

Y & R

Amman ◊ Jordan
PRINT

Creative Director Emad Khayyat
Art Director Glaucco Martines
Photographer Adriano Von Markendorf
Head of Stragety Gaitan De Mark
Account Director Ahmad Al Salem

Jordan Insurance Company:

Helmets

An open buckle helmet isn't a helmet.
When it comes to riding motorcycles, a huge percentage of the Jordanian riders use the helmet as an aesthetic accessory, or wear it to avoid a ticket from the traffic police. In these cases, the helmet is usually unbuckled, increasing the danger risk.

Un casco sin abrochar no es un casco.
A la hora de conducir una moto, un elevado porcentaje de los conductores jordanos utilizan el casco como accesorio estético o para evitar una multa de la policía de tráfico. En estos casos, a menudo el casco se lleva sin abrochar, aumentando los riesgos.

AN OPEN BUCKLE HELMET ISN'T A HELMET. SECURE YOURS BEFORE YOU RIDE. شركة التأمين الأردنية Jordan Insurance Company

AN OPEN BUCKLE HELMET ISN'T A HELMET. SECURE YOURS BEFORE YOU RIDE. شركة التأمين الأردنية Jordan Insurance Company

Alma

Miami ◇ USA
PRINT

Creative Chairman Luis Miguel Messianu
Chief Creative Officer Alvar Suñol
Art Director Christian Liu
Copywriter Juan Camilo Valdivieso
Producer Mimi Cossio
Senior Group Business Director Karla Kruger
VP Strategic Insights Angela Rodriguez
Photography-Postproduction & CGI Garrigosa Studio

How fast is fast?
"KINGSFORD"

On one hand, we have Kingsford® Match Light®, and on the other hand we have three creatures known for catching their prey in the blink of an eye.
What do Kingsford® Match Light® and these predators have in common? Lighting-fast speed.

Por un lado, tenemos Kingsford® Match Light®, y por otro lado tenemos tres criaturas conocidas por atrapar a sus presas en un abrir y cerrar de ojos.
¿Qué tienen en común Kingsford® Match Light® y estos depredadores? Velocidad de iluminación rápida.

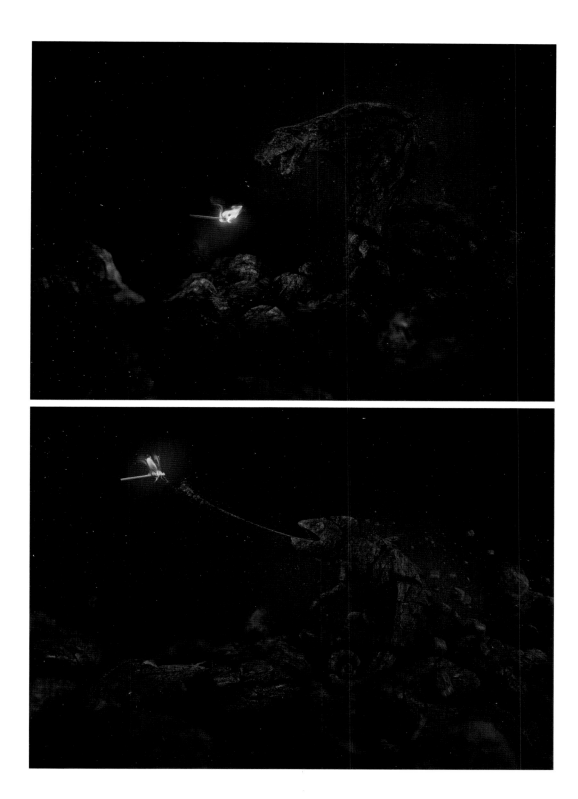

Lapiz debits

Bogotá ◊ Colombia
PRINT

Creative Director Artiom Gelvez Kostenko
Art Director Artiom Gelvez Kostenko
Copywriter Iana Goroba, Susana Gelvez Acosta
Illustrator Artiom Gelvez Kostenko

Nike

Unleash Your Animal
Libera tu animal.

UNLEASH
YOUR
ANIMAL

NIKE
JUST DO IT.

Y&R

São Paulo ◊ Brazil
PRINT

Chief Creative Officer Rui Branquinho
Head of Art Felipe Pavani
Creative Director Rui Branquinho
Art Director Kleyton Mourão
Copywriter Pedro Guerra e Roberto Pereira
Photographer Yongzhi Chu
Art Buyer Monica Beretta, Stephanie Wang
Print Production Ronaldo Cavalcante
Client Services Vivianne Brafmann
Media Gustavo Gaion, Marcello Bolla

Terrible

Visual impairment prevents us from seeing the most beautiful things and the worst atrocities as well.
Donating corneas therefore helps visually impaired individuals live a full life. We believe this is what makes us more tolerant human beings.

La discapacidad visual nos impide ver las cosas más bellas y las peores atrocidades también.
La donación de córneas ayuda a las personas con discapacidad visual a vivir una vida plena. Creemos que esto es lo que nos hace ser más humanos y tolerantes.

IT'S
HORRIBLE
TO
SEE IT.
IT'S
HORRIBLE
NOT TO
SEE IT.

Donate
Cornea.

Banco
de Olhos
Hospital
São
Paulo

Be a donor and inform your family.

IT'S
HORRIBLE
TO
SEE IT.
IT'S
HORRIBLE
NOT TO
SEE IT.

Donate
Cornea.

Banco
de Olhos
Hospital
São
Paulo

Be a donor and inform your family.

IT'S HORRIBLE TO SEE IT.

IT'S HORRIBLE NOT TO SEE IT.

Donate Cornea.

Banco de Olhos Hospital São Paulo

HOSPITAL UNIVERSITÁRIO UNIFESP

Be a donor and inform your family.
Info:+ 55 (11) 5572-3345 • hospitalsaopaulo.org.br/bancodeolhos • bohsunifesp@hotmail.com

Leo Burnett

Berlin ◊ Germany
PRINT

Chief Creative Officer Andreas Pauli
Copywriter Mark-Marcel Müller, Axel Tischer
Art Director Yigit Unan, Gabriel Mattar
Creative Director Gabriel Mattar, Axel Tischer
Production Company Photoby
Illustrator Zombie

Goodyear

Communicate the "Goodyear" technologies present in each tire in an unique way.
The campaign should resonate to tire dealers and consumers.

Presentamos la tecnología "Goodyear" presente en cada neumático de una manera única.
La campaña se plantea para cautivar a los distribuidores de neumáticos y a los consumidores.

J. Walter Thompson

Mexico City ◊ México
PRINT

Client Grupo Modelo
Chief Creative Officer Gabriel Vázquez
General Creative Direction Daniel García
Creative Director Martin Giudicessi
Art Director Martin Giudicessi
Copywriter Edgar Elorza
Client Services Alfredo Ramírez, Mateo Montes de Oca
Production Silvia Gómez
Illustrator Krisztianna Ortíz
Photographer Tim Tadder
Line Production Dahlia Snyder
Executive Production Gaby Rodríguez
Face / Body Painting Paul Roustan
Costume Julia Reeser
Design Sylva Welch & Lymari Millot
Makeup and Hairstyles Dezi V
Post Production Alexey Adamitsky

Day of the Dead for Cerveza Victoria

Victoria, the Mexican beer brand with 150 years, continues to build on its positioning "The Beer of Mexico". In this campaign, celebrating the Day of the Dead, Victoria and J. Walter Thompson Mexico reinterpret the Catrina, giving her an attractive and regional appearance that, with the talent of Tadder's lens, results in spectacular prints. Each of the 5 photographed Catrinas represent a different region of Mexico.
There is an "Azteca" Catrina, a "Poblana", a "Oaxaqueña", a "Tapatía" and a "Purepecha". To get insights of the culture of each region, the creative team researched the history of each of these places, observed their colours, textures, traditional clothing and hairstyles and their arts and crafts. Each Catrina was designed to have her own personality and to be very recognizable of the region she represents.

Victoria, marca de cerveza con 150 años de antigüedad, continúa su trayectoria para posicionarse como la "Cerveza de México". En esta campaña, para celebrar el Día de Muertos, Victoria y J. Walter Thompson México reinterpretan a la Catrina, proporcionándole un aspecto atractivo y regional, con el talento de la lente de Tadder, que resulta en unos anuncios impresos espectaculares. Cada una de las cinco Catrinas fotografiadas representa una región mexicana diferente.
Así, encontramos una Catrina "Azteca", una Catrina "Poblana", una Catrina "Oaxaqueña", una Catrina "Tapatía" y una Catrina "Purepecha". Para reflejar la cultura de cada región, el equipo creativo analizó la historia de cada uno de estos lugares y observó sus colores, texturas, vestimenta y peinados tradicionales, así como su artesanía. Cada Catrina se diseñó con una personalidad propia buscando su clara asociación con la región a la que representa.

Y & R

São Paulo ◊ Brazil
PRINT

Chief Creative Officer Rui Branquinho
Creative Director Rui Branquinho, Victor Sant'Anna
Art Director Leandro Câmara
Copywriter Christian Fontana
Illustrator Marco Cezar
Art Buyer Monica Beretta, Stephanie Wang
Print Production Elaine Carvalho, Ronaldo Cavalcante
Client Services Alessandro Cardoni, Diego Passos
Planner Ana Kuroki, Paulo Vita
Media Gustavo Gaion, Inajá Ramos

Inverse

With puzzling, stunning visuals, this campaign goes straight to the point to deliver the issue of not relying on official technical support for your Peugeot.

Con desconcertantes e increíbles elementos visuales, esta campaña trata de manera directa el hecho de no confiar en la asistencia técnica oficial para su Peugeot.

THE RIGHT PART DOESN'T WORK IN THE WRONG PLACE.
PEUGEOT TECHNICAL SUPPORT

MOTION & EMOTION

PEUGEOT

THE RIGHT PART DOESN'T WORK IN THE WRONG PLACE.
PEUGEOT TECHNICAL SUPPORT

MOTION & EMOTION

PEUGEOT

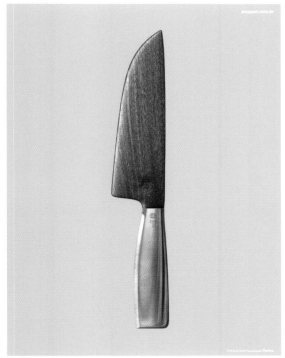

THE RIGHT PART DOESN'T WORK IN THE WRONG PLACE.
PEUGEOT TECHNICAL SUPPORT

MOTION & EMOTION

PEUGEOT

J. Walter Thompson

London ◊ UK
PRINT

Executive Creative Director Russell Ramsey
Creative Directors Christiano Neves, Paul Rizzello
Art Director Christiano Neves
Copywriter Paul Rizzello
Art Buyer Sue Clifford
Board Account Director Rafael Freitas
Creative Producer Laurie Carter
Photography Matt Holyoak

Objects

We're all a little bit paranoid about germs.
In spite of this, we all put things in our mouths without realising it – and without a thought for the last place it's been. By showing the journeys of these objects in single images, we can quickly remind people why they need a mouthwash that kills 99.9% of germs.

Todos somos un poco paranoicos con los gérmenes.
A pesar de esto, todos nos hemos puesto cosas en la boca sin darnos cuenta - y sin pensar en el último lugar que ha estado. Al mostrar los diferentes sitios donde han estado los objetos en imágenes individuales, recordamos rápidamente a la gente por qué necesitan un enjuague bucal que mate el 99,9% de los gérmenes.

WHERE'S YOUR MOUTH BEEN?

LISTERINE
COOL MINT

WHERE'S YOUR MOUTH BEEN?

LISTERINE
COOL MINT

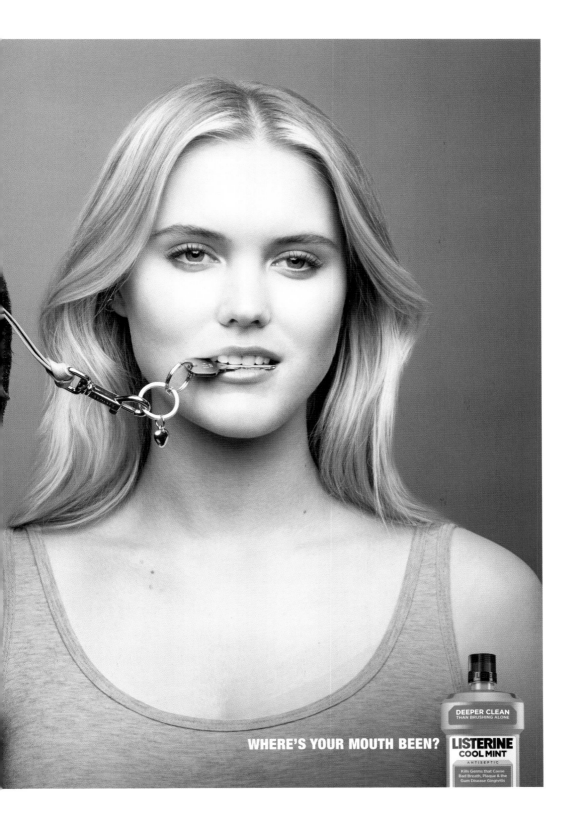

WHERE'S YOUR MOUTH BEEN?

61

Cheil

Kiev ◊ Ukraine
PRINT

Creative Director Vladyslava Denys
Art Director Iurii Gorbachevskyi
Copywriter Andrii Lazarenko
Photographer Andrey Demenyuk
Studio Magay Production
Producer Fedor Magay

Corrupt woman/man

While corrupt officials want to cover up their crimes,
they show them their way of life.
Reveal the corruption.

Mientras que los funcionarios corruptos quieren
encubrir sus crímenes, nos muestran su forma de vida.
Revelar la corrupción.

Corruption
must be
spotted

Stop it:
anticorruption.in.ua
TRANSPARENCY
INTERNATIONAL
Ukraine • www.ti-ukraine.org

CLM
BBDO

Boulogne Billancourt ◊ France
PRINT

Executive Creative Director Matthieu Elkaïm
Art Director Anthony Liétart
Copywriter Sébastien Duhaud
CEO Olivier Rippe
Managing Director Séverine Autret
Account Director Hicham Ghazaoui
Account Executive Charlotte Montrichard
Head of Art Buying Marie Bottin
CGI Jeremy Delhuvenne
Photographer Alex Murphy

Smart Cut In

Following the "Sorry" movie and the "Competitors" print campaign, BBDO Paris and Smart once again hit the spotlight through their new media and press campaign called "Cut in", which highlights the fact that there's only one smart that can take over another one.

Tras su anuncio "Sorry" (Perdón) y la campaña impresa "Competitors" (Competidores), BBDO Paris y Smart se unen de nuevo para crear su nueva campaña para prensa y medios "Cut in" (Corte), que destaca el hecho de que sólo un Smart puede dar el relevo a otro.

>> Only a smart can take the place of a smart.

>> Only a smart can take the place of a smart.

>> Only a smart can take the place of a smart.

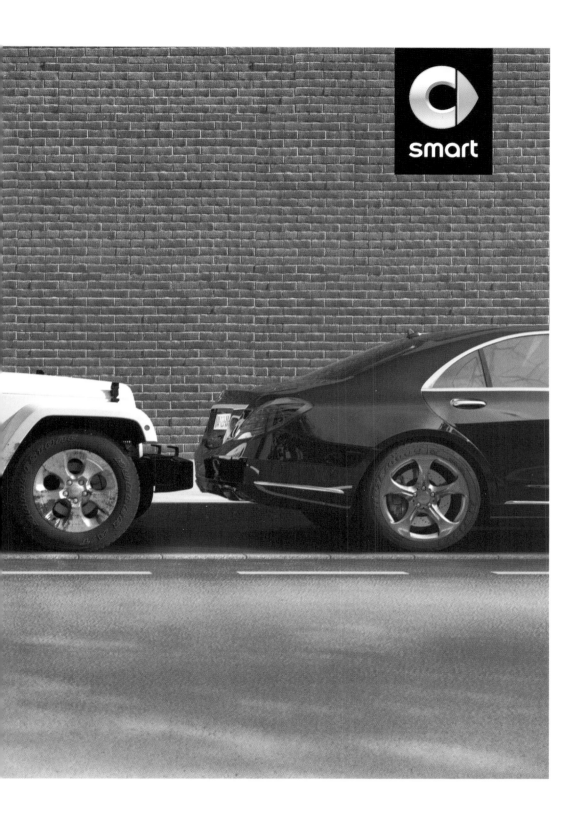

YR Prague

Prague ◊ Czech Republic
PRINT

Chief Creative Officer Jaime Mandelbaum
Creative Director Jaime Mandelbaum, Jaroslav Schovanec
Art Director Atila Martins
Copywriter Nathan Dills, Jaroslav Schovanec, Conor Barry, Dora Pruzincova
Designer Neil Johnston
Typography Neil Johnston
Photographer Miro Minarovych
Production Tomas Tomasek
3d Artist Marek Motalik

Harley WWII

To mark the anniversary of the end of the Second World War, we were asked to pay tribute and re-tell this incredible story of resistance.
An extremely local tale of defiance against oppression and outsmarting a larger opponent than yourself, proof that even in the darkest of times the human spirit always finds hope that one day freedom can prevail.

Para celebrar el aniversario del final de la Segunda Guerra Mundial, se nos pidió que rindiésemos tributo y volviésemos a contar esta increíble historia de resistencia.
Un relato extremadamente local de desafío a la opresión burlando a un adversario más grande que usted, para demostrar que incluso ante la mayor adversidad, el espíritu humano siempre encuentra esperanza para creer que algún día logrará la libertad.

THEY DIDN´T KNOW RIGHT FROM WRONG.

LUCKILY, THEY ALSO DIDN´T KNOW
AN EXHAUST PIPE FROM A HEATER.

During the Second World War,
Czech riders dismantled their bikes
and hid them amongst household objects
so they wouldn´t be confiscated
and used to continue fueling
the Nazi war machine.

These "parted out" bikes
became symbols of hope
that one day freedom would prevail
and they could be put back together
to reclaim their rightful home
— the open road.

A piece of freedom.

MOTOR
HARLEY-DAVIDSON
CYCLES

THE FÜHRER COULDN'T STOMP OUT HOPE BECAUSE
THE FÜHRER COULDN'T FIND OUR KICKSTARTER.

During the Second World War,
Czech riders dismantled their bikes and hid them
amongst household objects so they wouldn't
be confiscated and used to continue
fueling the Nazi war machine.

These "parted out" bikes became symbols
of hope that one day freedom would prevail
and they could be put back together to reclaim
their rightful home —
the open road.

A piece of freedom.

MOTOR HARLEY-DAVIDSON CYCLES

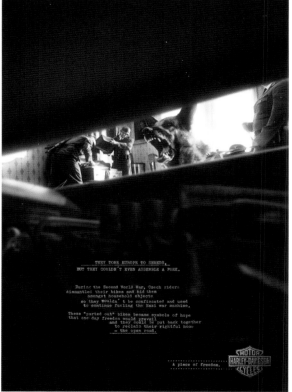

THEY TORE EUROPE TO SHREDS,
BUT THEY COULDN'T EVEN ASSEMBLE A FORK.

During the Second World War, Czech riders
dismantled their bikes and hid them
amongst household objects
so they wouldn't be confiscated and used
to continue fueling the Nazi war machine,

These "parted out" bikes became symbols of hope
that one day freedom would prevail
and they could be put back together
to reclaim their rightful home
— the open road.

A piece of freedom.

MOTOR HARLEY-DAVIDSON CYCLES

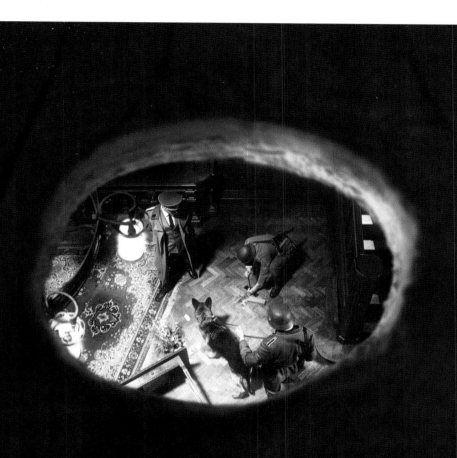

OUR ULTIMATE FREEDOM WAS HIDING RIGHT UNDER HIS NOSE.
NO, NOT IN THAT HORRIBLE MOUSTACHE.

During the Second World War, Czech riders dismantled
their bikes and hid them amongst household objects
so they wouldn t be confiscated

and used to continue fueling
the Nazi war machine.
....

These "parted out" bikes became symbols of hope
~~taht~~ that one day freedom would prevail
and they could be put back together
to reclaim their rightful home —
~~thé~~
the open road.

A piece of freedom.

Lapizdebits

Bogotá ◊ Colombia
PRINT

Creative Director Artiom Gelvez Kostenko
Art Director Artiom Gelvez Kostenko
Copywriter Alex Valyukh
Illustrator agelkos.com

W W F

The Earth drowns faster than nature adapts. Stop global warming.

La Tierra se ahoga más rápido de lo que la naturaleza se adapta. Stop al calentamiento global.

J. Walter Thompson

São Paulo ◊ Brazil
PRINT

Chief Creative Officer Ricardo John, Rodrigo Grau
Art Directors Humberto Fernandez, Pedro Coelho
Executive Creative Director Humberto Fernandez
Creative Director Mariana Borga
Copywriter Ricardo Ribeiro
Illustrator Diego Limberti
Photographer Regis Fernandez

Résumé

The AA has always been an important option in the fight against alcoholism. So, finding ways to bring more people to get their help is, and always will be, a marketing opportunity. But very often, ad agencies use this opportunity to point fingers and tell heavy drinkers the obvious: They are destroying their lives and the lives of their relatives. So, this time, we wanted to say something different, something that was true to the brand and that could be more helpful for them.
Our aim with the campaign is very simple: break the fear and shame barrier, making alcoholics feel comfortable and reassured to seek help and contact the AA. We want to show that the AA is comprised of alcoholics who have already been through everything an alcoholic can go through. That makes them the most qualified people to help other alcoholics. That is the message we want to convey, as objectively as possible.

AA siempre ha sido una opción importante para luchar contra el alcoholismo. De ahí que encontrar formas de atraer a más gente para ayudar es, y siempre será, una oportunidad de marketing. Pero con mucha frecuencia, las agencias de publicidad utilizan esta oportunidad para apuntar con el dedo y decir a los grandes consumidores de alcohol algo obvio: Que están destruyendo su vida y la de sus familiares. Así que esta vez queríamos decirles algo diferente, algo verdadero para la marca que les pudiera ayudar en mayor medida.
Nuestro objetivo con la campaña era muy sencillo: romper la barrera del miedo y la pena, haciendo que los alcohólicos se sientan cómodos y seguros de buscar ayuda y ponerse en contacto con AA. Queríamos demostrar que AA está formado por alcohólicos que han pasado por todo lo que puede pasar un alcohólico. Que son las personas más preparadas para ayudar a otros alcohólicos. Ese era el mensaje que queríamos hacer llegar, de la manera más objetiva posible.

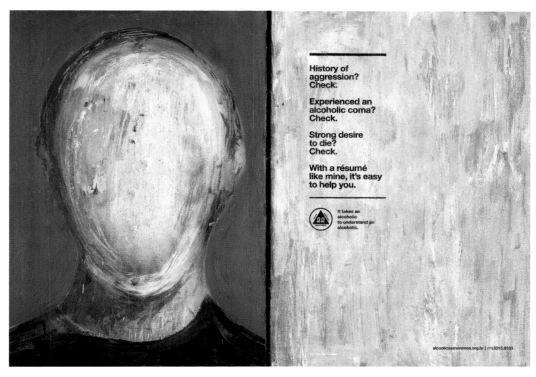

History of
aggression?
Check.

Experienced an
alcoholic coma?
Check.

Strong desire
to die?
Check.

With a résumé
like mine, it's easy
to help you.

It takes an
alcoholic
to understand an
alcoholic.

alcoolicosanonimos.org.br | (11) 3315.9333

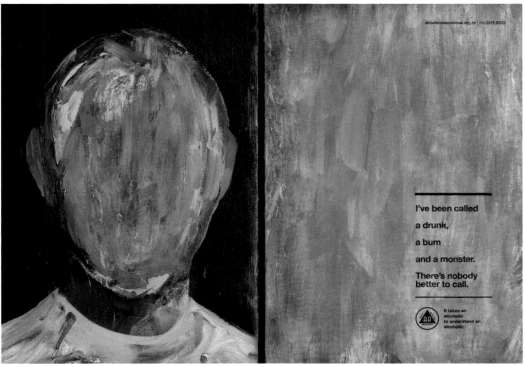

alcoolicosanonimos.org.br | (11) 3315.9333

I've been called

a drunk,

a bum

and a monster.

There's nobody
better to call.

It takes an
alcoholic
to understand an
alcoholic.

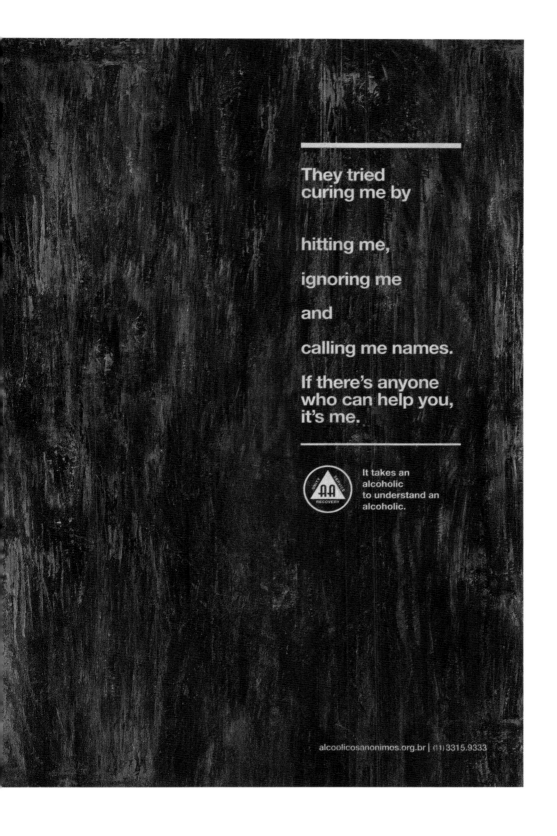

They tried
curing me by

hitting me,

ignoring me

and

calling me names.

If there's anyone
who can help you,
it's me.

It takes an
alcoholic
to understand an
alcoholic.

alcoolicosanonimos.org.br | (11) 3315.9333

Y&R

São Paulo ◊ Brazil
PRINT

Chief Creative Officer Rui Branquinho
Creative Director Rui Branquinho
Art Director Kleyton Mourão, Denon Oliveira
Copywriter Pedro Guerra
Illustrators Marcelo Braga, Rodolfo Martins
Photographer Shutterstock, Getty Images
Art Buyer Monica Beretta, Stephanie Wang
Print Production Elaine Carvalho, Ronaldo Cavalcante
Client Services Heloisa Mattos Pereira Guimarães
Planner Ana Kuroki
Media Gustavo Gaion, Marcello Bolla

Inside Out

What we eat penetrates the deepest layers of our body.
But there's an efficient way to get rid of what we don't want.

Lo que comemos penetra en las capas más profundas de nuestro cuerpo.
Pero hay una manera eficiente de deshacerse de lo que no queremos.

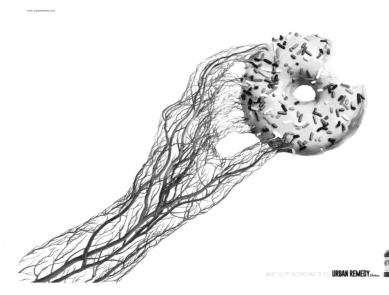

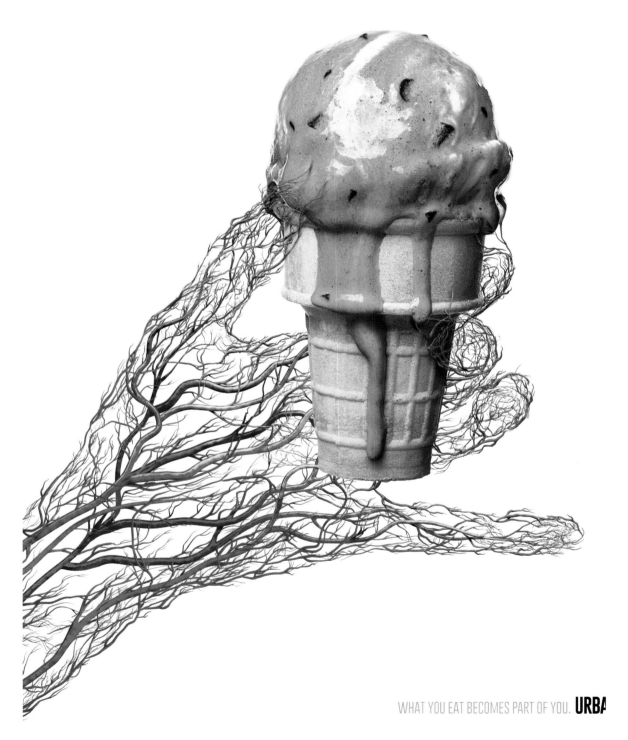

WHAT YOU EAT BECOMES PART OF YOU. **URBA**

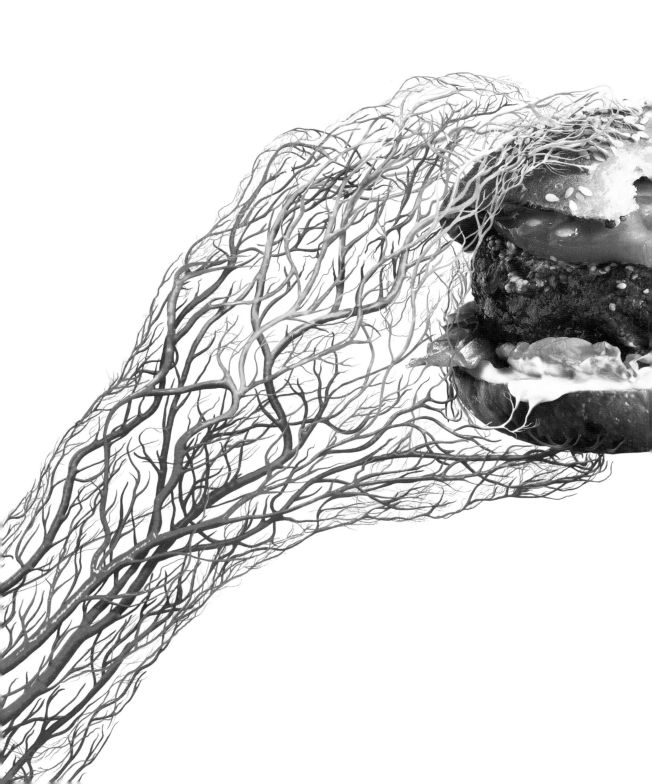

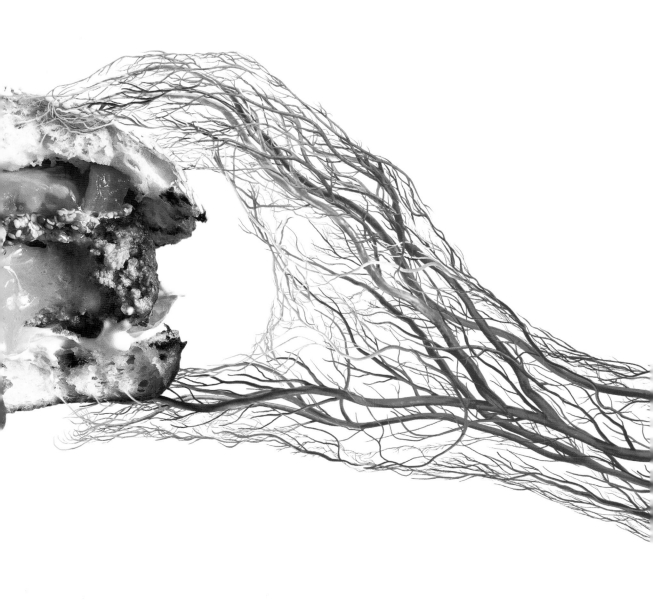

WHAT YOU EAT BECOMES PART OF YOU. **URBAN REMEDY** *Detox.*

Ogilvy & Mather

Frankfurt ◊ Germany
PRINT

Chief Creative Officer Dr. Stephan Vogel
Creative Directors Helmut Meyer, Lars Huvart,
Peter Strauss, Lothar Mueller
Art Director Christian Kuzman
Copywriter Christian Kuzman
Photographer Marc Wuchner
Art Buyers Franziska Günster, Pepe Freund
Account Yves Rosengart, David Henkel
Digital Artist Katja Dalek

Windstopper

To promote Schoeffel's windbreaker jackets, we created a print ad that showed people exactly what Schoeffel's jackets are capable of: keeping you warm by stopping any wind from coming through them. So we compared other textiles and the way they behave in stormy wind to the windbreaker jacket.

Para promover las chaquetas de viento de Schoeffel, creamos un anuncio impreso que mostraba exactamente lo que las chaquetas de Schoeffel son capaces de hacer: manteniendo el calor y evitando que el viento pase a través del tejido.
Así que comparamos otros tejidos expuestos a un viento tempestuoso y la eficacia de la chaqueta rompevientos.

Looma

Kiev ◊ Ukraine
PRINT

Creative Director Sergey Prokopchuk
Photographer Alexander Shabratko
Post-production Looma
CEO&Founder Irina Metneva
Project Manager Andrey Gorovoy
Make Up Anzhelika Voloshina

BRO

With BRO Men's care – you become a real magnet for women.

Con el cuidado de BRO hombres - te conviertes en un verdadero imán para las mujeres.

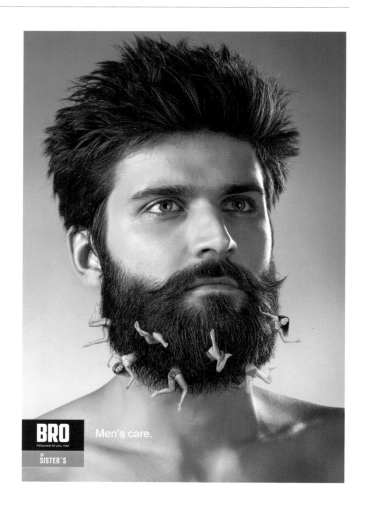

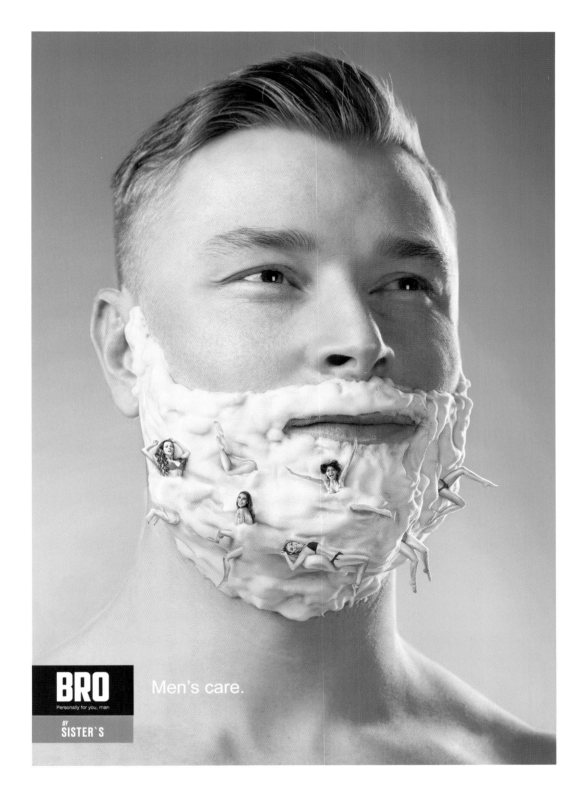

BRO
Personally for you, man

BY SISTER`S

Men's care.

TBWA

Zürich ◊ Switzerland
PRINT

Creative Director Bruce Roberts
Art Director Angelo Sciullo
Copywriter David Voges
Digital Tobias Jean
Art Buyer Ilonka Galliard
Account Stephan Lanz, Anna Magnaguagno
Photography-Postproduction & CGI Garrigosa Studio

McDonalds

Just in time for the UEFA Euro 2016, McDonald's offered a choice of three new Coca Cola glasses to accompany their hamburger and salad menus. These were a special edition, carrying the official EURO 2016 logo and were only available during the European Championships. TBWA\Zurich produced a poster campaign for McDonald's with the slogan "Das gibt's nicht alle Tage". The campaign focused on the limited period of the offer and the attractive design of the glasses.

Justo a tiempo para la Eurocopa de 2016, McDonald's ofrece uno de los tres nuevos vasos de Coca Cola por cada menú y menú de ensaladas. Dichos vasos, se han realizado con el diseño oficial EURO 2016 y sólo están disponibles durante el Campeonato de Europa. TBWA \ Zurich realizó una campaña de carteles para McDonald's bajo el lema "Das gibt's nicht alle Tage". La campaña se centró en una oferta con tiempo limitado y en el atractivo de los vasos.

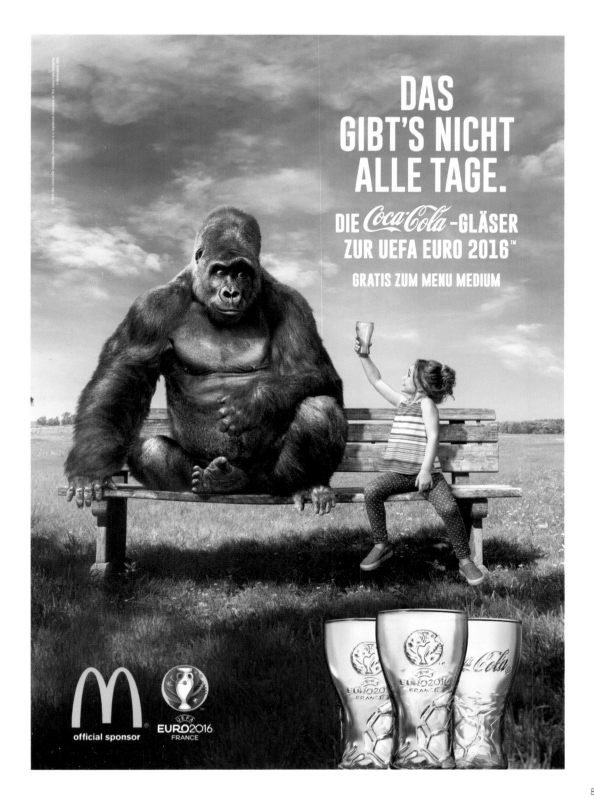

180 Amsterdam BV

Amsterdam ◊ The Netherlands
PRINT

Chief Creative Officer Al Moseley
Creative Director Martin Terhart / Martin Beswick
Art Director Ed Ryder
Copywriter Luke Stone
Producer Susan Cook
Managing Director Stephen Corlett
Account Manager Jim O'regan
Planner Ben Armistead
Project Manager Jo Borton / Eleanor Fitzgerald
Business Affairs Director Sarah Gough

The FCB Holiday 2015

This commercial 'Holiday' is the second instalment of Qatar Airways' much loved FC Barcelona campaign - The Team That Unites The World. In the commercial we get a glimpse into the 140 destinations that Qatar Airways now serve. We see the stars of FC Barcelona - Iniesta, Pique, Suarez, Neymar and Messi embark on a well earned end of season holiday. Flying around the world enjoying the inflight experience from Qatar Airways as they go, we join a fun and irreverent story of team-mates on holiday. We see Pique and Neymar teasing each other and messing around with suncream in the Maldives, we see Suarez displaying his skills as a Cowboy in Dallas, we see Iniesta and Pique enjoying a coffee in Paris before joining in with the local mimes, before finally we end up in Asia where Neymar and Messi use their famous skills and teamwork to defeat a gang of ninjas. The commercial finishes with the players returning home - dressed in all their holiday attire.

Este anuncio de "vacaciones" es la segunda entrega de la adorada campaña de Qatar Airways con el FC Barcelona - El equipo que une el mundo. En el anuncio podemos vislumbrar los 140 destinos a los que llega Qatar Airways en la actualidad. Vemos a las estrellas del FC Barcelona - Iniesta, Piqué, Suárez, Neymar y Messi embarcar rumbo a unas merecidas vacaciones de final de temporada. Volando por todo el mundo mientras disfrutan de la experiencia a bordo ofrecida por Qatar Airways, nos unimos a una divertida e irreverente historia de compañeros de vacaciones. Podemos ver a Piqué y Neymar bromeando y jugando con la crema solar en las Maldivas, a Suárez demostrando sus habilidades como cowboy en Dallas, a Iniesta y Piqué disfrutando de un café en París antes de unirse a los mimos locales, para terminar en Asia, donde Neymar y Messi utilizan sus capacidades y trabajo en equipo para derrotar a un grupo de ninjas. El anuncio finaliza con el regreso de los jugadores a casa, vestidos con su atuendo vacacional.

Kick-off your holiday to over 140 destinations worldwide.

A team that unites the world.
#FCBHolidays

World's 5-star airline.
qatarairways.com

Saatchi & Saatchi Wellness

New York ◇ USA
PRINT

Creative Director Kathy Delaney
Art Director Carolyn Gargano
Copywriter Scott Carlton
Illustrator Mike Perry
Photographer Nicolas Maloof
Art Buyer Erica Cassano

Street Fare

To increase community participation in volunteering and fundraising efforts, SSW championed a 360°
campaign for this homeless shelter, soup kitchen and food pantry.
Sometimes, just thinking about the struggles of those living on the street can be overwhelming.
For most people, it's often easier to put it out of their minds and move on.
The idea behind this project was to call attention to the everyday struggles faced by the hungry and
homeless in the place they actually occur the street. The approach was simple turn everyday potholes,
puddles and garbage into a vehicle for awareness by illustrating chalk-drawn faces around them.
Transit posters, online banners, TV commercials and video were developed to further spread the word.
Subsequently, the efforts grew virally as people worldwide created illustrations of their own, photographed,
posted and shared them on various social media sites.

Para aumentar la participación comunitaria en obras de voluntariado y la recaudación de fondos, SSW
realizó una campaña 360° para este albergue para personas sin hogar, comedor social y banco de alimentos.
En ocasiones, pensar en las dificultades de las personas que viven en la calle puede ser sobrecogedor.
Para la mayoría de la gente, a menudo es más sencillo sacarlo de su mente y pasar a otra cosa.
La idea que residía tras este proyecto era llamar la atención hacia la lucha cotidiana a la que se enfrentan las
personas hambrientas y sin hogar en el lugar en el que todo ocurre, la calle. El acercamiento fue sencillo,
convertir baches, charcos y basura cotidiana en un vehículo de concienciación dibujando caras con tiza
alrededor de ellos.
Para lograr mayor difusión, se elaboraron además pósteres de tránsito, banners online, anuncios de TV y
vídeos. Posteriormente, los esfuerzos se convirtieron en virales ya que personas de todo el mundo crearon
sus ilustraciones, las fotografiaron, publicaron y compartieron en diferentes redes sociales.

Serve
Marketing

Milwaukee ◊ USA
PRINT

Executive Creative Director Gary Mueller
Art Directors David Zimmerman, Nick Heiser, Casey Christian
Copywriter Stephanie Goldner
Photographers Nick Collura, Jeff Salzer
Retouchers Gina Ferrise, Anthony Giacomino
Account Executives Heidi Halperin, Matt Larson

Think Your Teen Life Won't Change?

In a collective effort to grow awareness and encourage prevention of teen pregnancies in Omaha, Serve Marketing has partnered with the Adolescent Health Project, an initiative of the Women's Fund of Omaha to launch the "Think Your Teen Life Won't Change?" campaign.
The campaign is intended to be a wake-up call to teens who don't think teen pregnancy will have a dramatic impact on their lives.
The effort comes in response to statistics from the Omaha Department of Public Health showing that Omaha has five zip codes with teen pregnancy rates that are up to three times the national average, and nearly double the rate for African American and Hispanic teens.
The bold campaign features the imagery of teen boys and girls participating in popular sports, all while a baby is attached to their chest. Headlines on ads that depict teens slam dunking a basketball, skateboarding, and blocking a soccer goal read, "Think your teen life won't change with a baby?" Copy then directs teens to visit the website, GetTheSexFactsOmaha.com, which offers resources to parents to help facilitate the conversation around sex and healthy sexual behavior.

En un esfuerzo colectivo para aumentar la concienciación y fomentar la prevención de embarazos durante la adolescencia en Omaha, Serve Marketing se ha asociado con el Adolescent Health Project, una iniciativa de Women's Fund of Omaha para lanzar la campaña "Think Your Teen Life Won't Change?" (¿Crees que tu vida de adolescente no va a cambiar?).
La campaña pretende llamar la atención de las adolescentes que creen que quedarse embarazada a su edad no va a tener un impacto dramático en su vida.
El esfuerzo pretende dar respuesta a las estadísticas del Departamento de Salud Pública de Omaha, que indican que cinco distritos postales de Omaha presentan una tasa de embarazo en adolescentes hasta tres veces superior a la media nacional, de casi el doble en el caso de adolescentes afroamericanas e hispanas.
Esta atrevida campaña muestra a chicos y chicas adolescentes practicando deportes populares} con un bebé en el pecho. El titular de los anuncios, en los que vemos a adolescente haciendo un mate, patinando o parando un gol, dice "Think your teen life won't change with a baby?" A continuación se dirige a los adolescentes al sitio web, GetTheSexFactsOmaha.com, en el que se ofrecen recursos para facilitar a los padres las conversaciones sobre sexo y comportamientos sexuales saludables.

THINK YOUR TEEN LIFE WON'T CHANGE WITH A BABY?

GetTheSexFactsOmaha.com

THINK YOUR TEEN LIFE WON'T CHANGE WITH A BABY?

GetTheSexFactsOmaha.com

THINK YOUR TEEN LIFE WON'T CHANGE WITH A BABY?

GetTheSexFactsOmaha.com

YR Prague

Prague ◊ Czech Republic
PRINT

Chief Creative Officer Jaime Mandelbaum
Creative Director Jaime Mandelbaum
Executive Creative Director Tereza Sverakova
Executive Managing Director Tomas Dvorak
Head of Art Atila Martins
Art Director Atila Martins
Copywriter Santiago Cosme, Jiri Kirchner
Designer Neil Johnston
Retouch Studio Carioca, Bucharest

The World Needs More Billionaires

The world is full of problems that need solving. Problems such as curing cancer, animals in danger of extinction, deforestation, etc... Unfortunately, the ability of the world to overcome these problems relies mainly on individual contributions that are often not enough to make a real impact. As a leading business magazine, Forbes has always stood behind world changers like Bill Gates, Warren Buffet, or Mark Zuckerberg who have made a pledge to use their wealth to make the world a better place. Forbes works to provide its readers with the insights they need to accomplish their goals and are now encouraging them to become the next generation of billionaires that help the world.

El mundo está lleno de problemas que necesitan una solución. Problemas como la cura del cáncer, los animales en peligro de extinción, la deforestación, etc.... Desafortunadamente, la capacidad del mundo para sobreponerse a estos problemas se basa principalmente en contribuciones individuales que a menudo resultan insuficientes para tener un impacto real. Como revista empresarial de éxito, Forbes siempre ha estado detrás de personas que pretenden cambiar el mundo como Bill Gates, Warren Buffet o Mark Zuckerberg, comprometidos con utilizar su riqueza para convertir el mundo en un lugar mejor. Forbes trabaja para proporcionar a sus lectores la perspectiva que necesitan para lograr sus objetivos y fomenta ahora su actuación para convertirse en la próxima generación de millonarios que ayuden al mundo.

THE COSTS OF CHANGING THE WORLD

ENDING POVERTY

$176 BILLION

PER YEAR

EDUCATION	HEALTH	WATER & SANITATION	GOVERNANCE & SECURITY	ENVIRONMENT	INFRASTRUCTURES	AGRICULTURE & FOOD SECURITY	ADMINISTRATION & DEBT RELIEF	HUMANITARIAN
$12.6 BN	$17.2 BN	$6.3 BN	$17.9 BN	$5.2 BN	$15.7 BN	$12.5 BN	$75.2 BN	$13.1 BN

THE WORLD NEEDS MORE BILLIONAIRES

Forbes

THE MOST POWERFUL PHILANTHROPISTS

Y & R

São Paulo ◊ Brazil
PRINT

Chief Creative Officer Rui Branquinho
Head of Art Felipe Pavani
Creative Director Rui Branquinho
Art Director Thiago de Melo
Copywriter Rodrigo Mendonça
Illustrator Gabriel Bueno
Image bank Getty Images Campo, Árvores
Image bank LatinStock
Art Buyer Monica Beretta, Stephanie Wang
Print Production Ronaldo Cavalcante
Account Director Heloisa Guimarães
Media Gustavo Gaion, Marcello Bolla

Roots

By using aerial images of rivers that resemble the roots of a tree, we show that they are fundamental for the existence of nature and life.

Mediante el uso de imágenes aéreas de ríos que se asemejan a las raíces de un árbol, mostramos que son fundamentales para la existencia de la naturaleza y la vida.

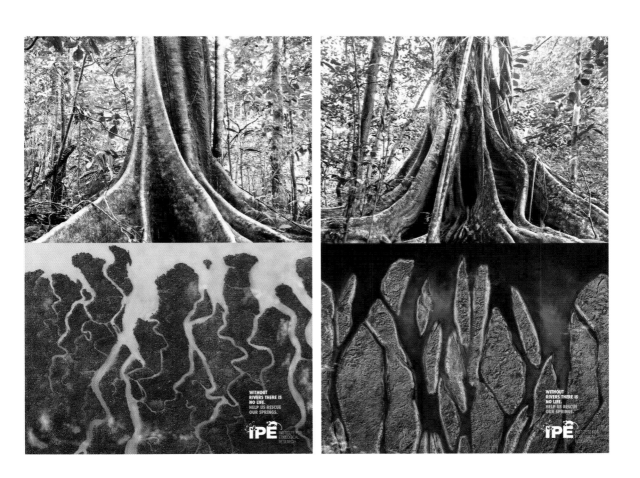

WITHOUT
RIVERS THERE IS
NO LIFE.
HELP US RESCUE
OUR SPRINGS.

iPÊ INSTITUTE FOR ECOLOGICAL RESEARCH

WITHOUT
RIVERS THERE IS
NO LIFE.
HELP US RESCUE
OUR SPRINGS.

iPÊ INSTITUTE FOR ECOLOGICAL RESEARCH

Michurin

Kiev ◊ Ukraine
PRINT

Creative Director Dima Bolsunovsky
Art Director/Copywriter Sergey Prokopchuk
CGI Looma

WSP Italy: Serve and Protect

4 medieval knights with round shields symbolize 4 tough car wheels, that will serve you and protect from any road difficulties.

4 caballeros medievales con escudos redondos simbolizan 4 ruedas de coche resistentes, que le servirán y protegerán de cualquier dificultad del camino.

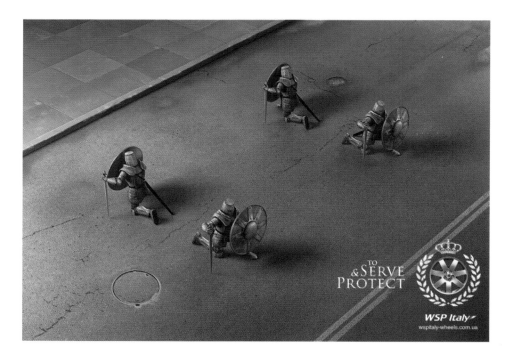

TO
&SERVE
PROTECT

Leo Burnett

Dubai ◊ UAE
PRINT

Chief Creative Director Bechara Mouzannar
Executive Creative Director Andre Nassar
Art Director Bruno Bomediano / Victor Toyofuku / Robison Mattei
Creative Director Bruno Bomediano
Copywriter Wayne Fernandes
Photographer Daniel Botezatu / Littematter

McDonals:
Chinese, Indian, Arabic Restaurants

We were briefed to create a campaign to tell people that McDonald's is open for business round the clock.
We set out to show the plain and simple truth. We showed the city by night. Asleep. With just the McDonald's 24-hour signage reflecting off of shut restaurant windows.

Recibimos información para crear una campaña para decirle a la gente que McDonald's está abierto las veinticuatro horas del día para negocios.
Nos propusimos mostrar simplemente la verdad, mostramos la ciudad de noche, dormida, destacando sólo la señal de 24 horas de McDonald's reflejándose en las ventanas cerradas del restaurante.

J. Walter Thompson

London ◊ UK
PRINT

Creative Director David Masterman
Art Director Claudia Southgate
Copywriter Claudia Southgate
Account Director Charlie Martyn
Account Manager Max Sullivan
Project Manager Stephanie West
Retouching Les Wilson

Care for the Wild International

Right now, badgers are trapped and shot by DEFRA contractors because of Government's policy. The new ad created by JWT London, which shows a dramatic take on a badger with a gun to his head, aims to expose the brutality of these actions.

En este momento, los tejones están atrapados y fusilados por contratistas DEFRA debido a la política del Gobierno. El nuevo anuncio creado por JWT London, que muestra una dramática toma de un tejón con una pistola en la cabeza, pretende exponer la brutalidad de estas acciones.

Cheil

Kiev ◊ Ukraine
PRINT

Creative Director Vladyslava Denys
Art Director Iurii Gorbachevskyi
Copywriter Alexander Valyukh
Account Director Iryna Kochubey
Account Manager Miroslava Chernaya

Lungs

Thanks to hi-tech filters, Samsung vacuum cleaners clean even the air in the room during cleaning.

Gracias a los filtros de alta tecnología, las aspiradoras de Samsung limpian incluso el aire den la habitación durante la limpieza.

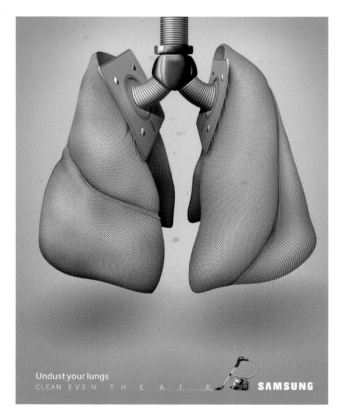

New !

Vilnius ◊ Lithuania
PRINT

Creative Director Tomas Ramanauskas
Account Deimante Statinyte
Copy Tomas Markauskas, Žygimantas Kudirka
Art Regis Pranaitis
Photographer Tomas Kauneckas
Retoucher Gintare Maciuliene

15 min

15min. It is one of the largest news websites in Lithuania.
The summer campaign invites to spend a little bit of
holiday time with the main international news heroes.

15 minutos. Es uno de los sitios web de noticias más
conocido de Lituania.
La campaña de verano invita a pasar un poco de tiempo
de vacaciones con los principales héroes de las noticias
internacionales.

15 | Stay with news, even on holiday

Stay with news, even on holiday

15 Stay with news, even on holiday

DDB

Berlin ◊ Germany
PRINT

Chief Creative Officer Eric Schoeffler
Creative Directors Tomas Tulinius, Stephan Schaefer
Art Director José Gomes
Copywriter Pedro Lourenço
Art Buyer Isabell Rusch
Agent PAM - Mirjam Böhm
Photography-Postproduction & CGI Garrigosa Studio

Ostrich

We were asked to promote the launch of the new Volkswagen Scirocco GTS, an even sportier version of the fast Scirocco, with an attention-grabbing print ad.
The message: if it's fast, it should also look like that. To create the perfect metaphor for the Scirocco GTS campaign, we depicted a fast animal that covers itself with the coat of an even faster animal.
The result is an image that shows an ostrich in a leopard suit. This image clearly communicates what customers can expect from the new Scirocco GTS: an even faster version of an already fast car.

Se nos pidió que promocionásemos el lanzamiento del nuevo Volkswagen Scirocco GTS, una versión aún más deportiva del rápido Scirocco, con un anuncio impreso que llamase la atención.
El mensaje: si es rápido, también debe parecerlo. Para crear la metáfora perfecta para la campaña del Scirocco GTS, mostramos un animal rápido que se cubre con la piel de un animal aún más rápido.
El resultado es una imagen que muestra un avestruz con un traje de leopardo. Esta imagen comunica de manera clara lo que los clientes pueden esperar del nuevo Scirocco GTS: una versión todavía más rápida de un coche ya rápido.

Kitchen
Leo Burnett

Oslo ◊ Norway
PRINT

Art Directors Ole Henrik Stubberud, Anne Gravingen
Copywriter Bendik Romstad
Executive Producer Lise Marie Mørkved
Account Manager Karoline Nybakk
Graphic Designer Kamilla Ellingsen
Motion Designer Adam Grüner
Community Manager Mats Abrahamsen
Studio Gimpville AS
Photo Aksel Jermstad, byAksel
Producer Lars Erik Hansen
Prop Nina Bjerch-Andresen
Puppet-maker Merete Bostrøm
Retouch Jan Svalland, Kristian Dale, Simon Nyhus
VFX Animation Alf Martin Løvvold

Bad Teddy

The number of children with asthma and allergies is increasing at an alarming rate.
Dust induces the risk of developing asthma, especially for children because their lungs are not fully developed yet.
The core idea was to emphasize for parents that cute, dusty stuffed animals actually could be very dangerous – but also letting them now there is a simple solution to the problem.
Thanks to a wide cover of the campaign and spreads in social media we had great PR value.
The campaign had a reach of 642 million people worldwide. The media value is 5,9 million USD - with a total media spending of 9800 USD.

El número de niños con asma y alergias aumenta a una velocidad alarmante.
El polvo incrementa el riesgo de desarrollar asma, especialmente en el caso de los niños, cuyos pulmones aún no han terminado de desarrollarse.
La idea principal era hacer saber a los padres que los bonitos y polvorientos animales de peluche en realidad pueden ser muy peligrosos, informándoles además de que la solución al problema es sencilla.
Gracias a la amplia cobertura de la campaña y su difusión en las redes sociales, hemos obtenido un gran valor de RRPP.
La campaña ha llegado a 642 millones de personas de todo el mundo. El valor medio sería de 5,9 millones de USD, con un gasto medio total de 9.800 USD.

**TEDDY BEARS CAN
BE DANGEROUS**

Collectors of dust in children's rooms can provoke asthma
and allergies. Wash stuffed animals four times a year.
Find more preventive tips at lhl.no/stovsamlere

LHL Asthma and allergy

TEDDY BEARS CAN BE DANGEROUS

Collectors of dust in children's rooms can provoke asthma
and allergies. Wash stuffed animals four times a year.
Find more preventive tips at lhl.no/stovsamlere

LHL Asthma and allergy

Leo Burnett

Frankfurt ◊ Germany
PRINT

Chief Creative Officer Andreas Pauli
Executive Creative Director Christoph Riebling
Creative Directors Benjamin Merkel, Helge Kniess
Senior Copywriter Christian Urbanski
Senior Art director Thomas Koch
Design Michael Fluhr
Client Service Director Martin Krauter
Group Account Director Pia Schütz
Creative Technologist Viktor Kislovskij
Social Media Consultant Felix Schrader

Design your time

In December, thousands of internet users followed the call to submit images for the Samsung "Design Your Time" campaign. The participants created an individual watch face for every specific minute.
They drew, wrote and painted – the result are thousands of completely unique dials for the Samsung Smartwatch. The most original ones were selected and are now part of the first user-generated Samsung Watchface. With the app, every glance at the Gear S2 or Gear S2 classic promises a surprise because the dial changes every minute. 1440 times a day.

En diciembre, miles de usuarios de Internet respondieron a la solicitud de envío de imágenes para la campaña "Design Your Time" (Diseña tu tiempo) de Samsung. Los participantes crearon una esfera de reloj individual para cada minuto específico.
Dibujaron, escribieron y pintaron, el resultado:
Miles de esferas completamente únicas para el Samsung Smartwatch. Las más originales fueron seleccionadas y ahora forman parte de la primera Samsung Watchface generada por los usuarios. Con la aplicación, cada mirada al Gear S2 o Gear S2 classic promete ser una sorpresa, porque la esfera cambia cada minuto. 1.440 veces al día.

Outdoor Advertising

"Publicidad de Exterior"

"Outdoor" advertising is that in which public spaces are used to display messages to an undetermined audience.
The formats used include posters, advertising hoardings, illuminated signs, banners and all other types of media which can be installed in public places, at sports venues, shows and events, etc.

This type of advertising, clearly visible and often entertaining, has become part of our everyday surroundings. In other words, it is now widely accepted, stands out and adds to the appearance of the locations where it is displayed. Agencies are well aware that it offers an unbeatable advertising space for new products, reaching a far wider audience than other formats.

Se considera publicidad de "exterior" a aquella que utiliza lugares públicos para desarrollarse y es dirigida a un público indeterminado.
Está formada por carteles, vallas publicitarias, rótulos luminosos, banderolas y todos aquellos soportes que se instalan en lugares públicos o donde se desarrollan espectáculos, eventos culturales, encuentros deportivos, etc.

Este tipo de publicidad vistosa y divertida, pasa a forma parte del entorno. Es decir, es aceptada, y luce muy bien en los lugares en los que tiene representación. Las agencias saben que comunicar en espacios públicos sus novedades, es un marco publicitario incomparable para sus objetivos, por lo que mostrar su publicidad puede, y suele llegar a muchas mas persona.

The Classic Partnership

Dubai ◊ UAE
AMBIENT

Executive Creative Director Alok Gadkar
Creative Directors Satyen Adhikari, Alok Gadkar
Art directors Vishal Vinekar, Satyen Adhikari
Copywriters Nilesh Naik, Satyen Adhikari
Illustrator Vishal Vinekar
Head of Production Vitthal Deshmukh
Production Manager Shankar Chidambaram
General Manager Alok Gadkar
Group Head Pulkit Vasisht
Retoucher Devraj Shriyan
Production House RGB
Senior Producer Ashwin Menon
DOP Prasad Paniker
Photographer Nasir Rauf

The Nazar Intiative
Design that made them see better

Dubai's construction workers are exposed to sun and sand, round the year. Light-toned surfaces like sand have high Albedo that can cause acute damage to the eyes. Hence, we wanted the workers to undergo a visual acuity test. However, the challenge was, most of these workers are illiterate. So we designed an eye chart using icons of equipment used in the construction industry. These eye charts, which worked as effectively as the "Snellen Eye Chart", were distributed to workers across Dubai. The workers underwent a visual acuity test with the help of these charts as they could easily identify the icons. Those workers with poor eyesight went to an Aster Clinic for a thorough eye check up. Over 7.000 workers took the test, 33% of them suffered from poor vision and received free eye glasses. Several workers pledged to get their eyes checked at least once a year. Thus we ended up creating a design language that can be adapted and implemented across illiterate communities around the world.

Los trabajadores de la construcción de Dubai están expuestos al sol y la arena durante todo el año. Las superficies de colores claros como la arena tienen un alto albedo, de ahí que puedan provocar daños graves en los ojos. Por eso queríamos que los trabajadores se sometiesen a un examen de agudeza visual. No obstante, el desafío era que la mayoría de estos trabajadores son analfabetos. Esto nos llevó a diseñar una tabla optométrica utilizando iconos en forma de objetos utilizados en el sector de la construcción. Esta tabla, que ha funcionado de manera tan eficaz como la "Tabla de Snellen", se distribuyó entre los trabajadores de Dubai. Dado que podían identificar los iconos fácilmente, estos realizaron el examen de agudeza visual con la ayuda de la tabla. Los trabajadores con visión deficiente acudieron a la Clínica Aster para someterse a un examen más profundo. Más de 7.000 trabajadores realizaron el examen, 33% de los cuales padecían de visión deficiente y recibieron gafas de manera gratuita. Numerosos trabajadores prometieron revisarse la vista al menos una vez al año. Así, acabamos creando un idioma de diseño que podía adaptarse e implementarse entre las comunidades sin alfabetizar de todo el mundo.

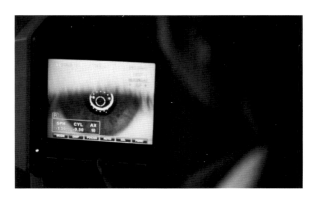

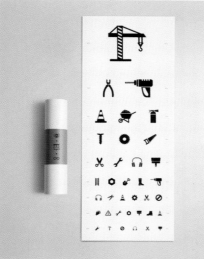

Serve Marketing

Milwaukee ◊ USA
OUTDOOR

Creative Director Gary Mueller
Art Director Mitch Markussen
Copywriter Mike Holicek
Photographer Anthony Giacomino
Account Executive Heidi Sterricker, Lauren Wagner

Human Trafficking

Milwaukee has experienced an alarming surge in sex trafficking, in which the average age a child is first sold for sex is just 13. To illustrate the inhuman nature of this industry, vending machines were placed in public areas showing teenage girls for sale. Messaging directed onlookers to a website where they could learn warning signs and ways to protect their children. A press conference followed, bringing the crisis of human trafficking to its widest audience to date.

Milwaukee ha experimentado un alarmante aumento del tráfico sexual, con niños de una media de sólo 13 años vendidos como objetos sexuales. Para ilustrar la inhumana naturaleza de este sector, se colocaron máquinas de vending en las que se vendía a chicas adolescentes en lugares públicos. El mensaje dirigía a los observadores a un sitio web en el que pueden conocer signos de reconocimiento y formas de proteger a sus hijos. Posteriormente se celebró una conferencia de prensa, llevando la crisis del tráfico de personas al público más amplio hasta la fecha.

J. Walter Thompson

London ◊ UK
OUTDOOR

Creative Director Dave Dye
Creatives Senan Lee, Pansy Aung
Illustrators Jordan Cheung, Toby Leigh,
Dave Anderson, Paul Bower.

Record Store Day

The idea is to encourage people to support their independent record stores and buy vinyl locally.
As an agency full of music obsessives JWT London offered to help promote Record Store Day.

PROBLEM:
The big question was how can we spread awareness without a budget for media?
Social media was obviously the channel, but we had two concerns;
1: How do we create something that people would engage with and share?
2: Is seeing something on your feed just too far from the stores themselves, both literally and metaphorically?
We could create something cool and shareable that made you feel better about vinyl, but would it get you to a store?
We need to be nearer to the point of purchase.
We need to divert people on their day to day journeys to visit their local record store.
So what's our media?

SOLUTION:
Other local businesses.
We enlist the other local businesses to show their support for Record Store Day by putting posters in their windows.
It would be good for them because they would be demonstrating their support for local, independent businesses like themselves.
It would be good for us because it's free media, close to the point of purchase.

IDEA:
Just writing 'Support your local record store' on posters with a date underneath wouldn't work.
We needed an idea that would;
a) Attract attention.
b) Make the businesses that put them up feel good.
c) Create a positive vibe around Record Store Day.
d) Announce the date.
e) Produce something cool enough that people would photograph and share.
We decided that the more we personalised each poster the prouder each business would feel.
But we also needed a theme to connect the posters, so that every window people saw would connect to the last.
Graphically we asked ourselves what objects that were in these local businesses that look like records?
A pizza, liquorice wheel, top view of a bowl of noodles, a pool 8 ball, etc.
Next we enlisted the creative images to capture a bunch of these 'ideas' visually; illustrators, photographers and artists.

RESULT:
The most successful Record Store Day to date.

La idea era animar a la gente a apoyar a las tiendas de discos independientes y comprar vinilos a nivel local.

Como agencia repleta de obsesionados por la música, JWT London se ofreció a ayudar en la promoción del Record Store Day.

PROBLEMA:

La gran pregunta era cómo lograr la concienciación sin presupuesto para medios.

Sin duda las redes sociales eran el canal a utilizar, pero existían dos preocupaciones:

1: ¿Cómo crear algo con lo que la gente se comprometiera y que pudieran compartir?

2: ¿Ver algo en las redes sociales está muy lejos de las tiendas en sí, tanto literal como metafóricamente hablando?

Podíamos crear algo atractivo y que se pudiera compartir que le hiciera sentirse mejor con los vinilos, pero ¿esto le llevaría hasta la tienda?

Necesitábamos estar más cerca del punto de compra.

Necesitábamos animar a la gente a visitar las tiendas de discos locales en su día a día.

¿Qué medio debíamos utilizar entonces?

SOLUCIÓN:

Otros negocios locales.

Nos pusimos en contacto con otros negocios locales para que mostrasen su apoyo al Record Store Day colocando pósteres en sus escaparates.

Para ellos era una buena iniciativa porque demostraban su apoyo por los negocios locales independientes como el suyo.

Para nosotros porque se trata de un medio gratuito, cercano a los puntos de compra.

IDEA:

Escribir simplemente 'Support your local record store' (Apoye a las tiendas de discos locales) en los pósteres seguido de una fecha no funcionaría.

Necesitábamos una idea que:

a) Llamase la atención.

b) Hiciese a los negocios que colocasen los pósteres sentirse bien.

c) Crease una atmósfera positiva en torno al Record Store Day.

d) Anunciase la fecha.

e) Mostrase algo lo suficientemente atractivo para que la gente lo fotografiase y lo compartiese.

Así, decidimos que cuanto más personalizásemos cada póster, más orgullosos se sentirían los negocios.

Pero también necesitábamos una temática que conectase los pósteres entre sí, para que cada escaparate que alguien viese estuviese relacionado con el anterior.

Nos preguntamos qué objetos de los negocios locales se parecían a los discos a nivel gráfico.

Una pizza, una rueda de regaliz, un bol de noodles visto desde arriba, una bola de billar, etc.

A continuación, nos centramos en las imágenes creativas para capturar diversas "ideas" a nivel visual; ilustradores, fotógrafos y artistas.

RESULTADO:

El Record Store Day con más éxito hasta la fecha.

RECORD STORE DAY:
16.04.16 - SUPPORTED
BY

PHONICA - 51 Poland St. SISTER RAY - 75 Berwick St. RECKLESS RECORDS - 30 Berwick St.
IF MUSIC - 12 D'Arblay St. SOUNDS OF THE UNIVERSE - 7 Broadwick St. RECORD STORE DAY

RECORD STORE DAY:
16.04.16 - SUPPORTED
BY

RECORD STORE DAY:
16.04.16 - SUPPORTED
BY

Kitchen
Leo Burnett

Oslo ◊ Norway
OUTDOOR

Art Directors Torkel Bjørnstad Sveen, Per Erik Jarl
Copywriters Ola Øvrelid, Christian Hygen, Maren Gimnes
Senior Designers Pia Lystad, Marianne Sæther
Motion Animation Adam Grüner
Film Editor Aasmund Amundsen
Digital Marketing Specialist Mats Abrahamsen
Head of Innovation Tom Andre Engli Andersson
Designers Eirik Waldermar Fjerdingstad, Kamilla Ellingsen
Consultant and Creative Producer Aram Zarkoob
Account Manager Karoline Nybakk
Program Developer Simen Øian Gjermundsen

Void
Developer and Designer Kristian Stoveland
Designer Anders Nærø Tangen
Developer and Designer Bjørn Gunnar Staal
Architect Joakim Wiig Hoen
Account Manager Mikkel Lehne

Computational design studio

Pudder Agency
Photographer Einar Aslaksen

Velcrux
DOP velc
DOP Herman Stenerud

Secret Num8rs

The secret numbers was a project to create buzz around the upcoming Kraftwerk concerts in Oslo. The only problem was that we couldn't mention Kraftwerk, the concerts or the venue. Our solution was to create something that was viewable for everyone, but only made sense for the true Kraftwerk fans.
8 days before the release of the concerts, 8 mysterious numbers appeared in different locations in Oslo. Every day the numbers moved to new locations, bringing them closer to the National Opera house. On the eight day the installation became complete, and the news that Kraftwerk were playing 8 concerts, each dedicated to one of the 8 official Kraftwerk albums.
The numbers were equipped with ultrasonic sensors, and passers-bye triggered a sound especially made by Kraftwerk for this project. When the installation became complete everyone could walk their own version of the iconic song Numbers by Kraftwerk.

El proyecto de los "números secretos" buscaba promocionar los próximos conciertos de Kraftwerk en Oslo. El único problema era que no podíamos mencionar ni Kraftwerk, ni los conciertos ni el lugar de celebración. Nuestra solución fue crear algo que todo el mundo pudiese ver pero sólo los fans de Kraftwerk pudiesen reconocer.
Ocho días antes de dar a conocer los conciertos, aparecieron ocho números misteriosos en diferentes lugares de Oslo. Cada día los números cambiaban de ubicación, acercándose cada vez más a la Ópera de Oslo. El octavo día la instalación se completó y se anunció que Kraftwerk iba a ofrecer ocho conciertos, cada uno de ellos dedicado a uno de los ocho álbumes oficiales del grupo.
Los números se equiparon con sensores ultrasónicos, que emitían un sonido creado especialmente por Kraftwerk para este proyecto al paso de los transeúntes. Cuando se finalizó la instalación, cualquier podía crear su propia versión de la icónica canción de Kraftwerk "Numbers".

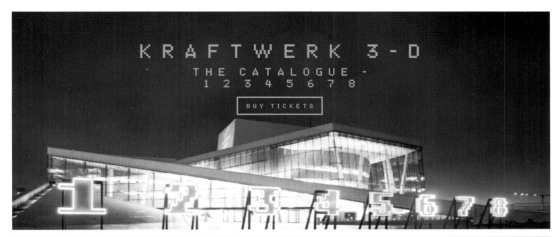

<title>

<TheSecret Num8rs>

</title>

The Secret Num8rs was made to create buzz around the upcoming Kraftwerk concerts in Oslo. Our solution was to create something that was viewable for everyone, but only made sense for the true Kraftwerk fans.

8 days before the release of the concerts, 8 mysterious numbers appeared in different locations in Oslo. Every day the numbers moved to new locations, bringing them closer to the National Opera house. On the eight day the installation became complete, everyone could walk their own version of the iconic vocoder sequence from the song Numbers by Kraftwerk.

The installations were equipped with ultrasonic sensors and the sounds were made by Kraftwerk exclusively for this project.